Getting Married and Staying That Way

Deven Jones

Getting Married and Staying That Way

Copyright © 2017 by Deven Jones

No part of this publication may be reproduced, stored in a retrieval system, distributed, or transmitted in any form or by any means including electronic, mechanical, digital, photocopy, recording, or any other without the prior written permission of the publisher/author. The authorized purchaser has been granted a nontransferable, nonexclusive, and noncommercial right to access and view this publication in any form. The purchaser agrees to do so only in accordance with the terms of use under which it is purchased or transmitted. Participation in or encouragement of piracy of copyrighted materials in violation of author's/publisher's rights is strictly prohibited.

ISBN-10: 0-9989816-0-5

ISBN-13:978-0-9989816-0-4

Library of Congress Control Number: 2017909590

First Printing: 2017

Editing by: Sasha Tropp

Cover by: Dropdeaddesigns.com

Contact: Deven Jones @

Devenspov.com

Printed in the United States.

"What therefore God hath joined together, let not man put asunder." (Matthew 19:6)

Contents

Introduction: Elements for a Healthy Marriage………..…….......9

1. The Honeymoon Phase………..…13

2. Marriage After the Honeymoon.16

3. No One Is a Mind Reader…...….23

4. Mind Your Mouth: Once You Say It, You Can't Take It Back ………..31

5. Pick Your Battles…………..…..37

6. Putting In Work: Quality Time, Compromise, and Intimacy…..…….44

7. Gender Roles……………..…...…50

8. For Better or For Worse………...59

9. Outside Influences……….……..66

10. Always Give Praise and Show Appreciation............................…..77

11. Incorporate the Fruits of the Spirit into Your Relationship................…....79

Conclusion...........…................…81

Acknowledgements..….....…...…....87

Notes...….......…....................…91

Note: The scriptures used throughout the book were taken from the King James Version of the Bible.

INTRODUCTION
Elements For A Healthy Marriage

When we're young, we are taught a lot of different things to help prepare us for what we may face as adults. We learn things in school and from our peers, we learn from behaviors displayed by the adults around us, and some people learn things from the church that they attend. Eventually we take what we have learned and apply it to our adult lives. What happens when the adults that you were exposed to did not set good examples related to having a healthy marriage? What happens when there are no discussions about how to conduct yourself in a marriage? The result is people who don't see the benefit of marriage, unhappily married couples, or divorce. So, how can couples who have chosen to get married stay that way?

Marriage can be a wonderful experience, as long as you keep in mind that you are each an individual, and that no one is perfect. Marriage is a process involving trial and error and learning how to share a space with the one that you love. You are supposed to learn and grow together. There will be ups and downs, good days and bad days, and you won't always see eye to eye. This is normal.

There are several elements that can help maintain a healthy marriage: communication, compromise, patience, respect, prayer, and a willingness to grow and change in a positive way. Communication is a must, as the lack thereof, can destroy a marriage. Since marriage is a two-way street between two individuals, compromise is necessary. You can't always have things your way. There must be compromise, along with patience and respect. Your body language, along with what you say and how you say it, all show your level of respect for your spouse. Another element is prayer. Including God in your relationship will benefit your marriage greatly. God knows you best, and he is the only one who can get someone to change for the better. As you grow together, it is wise to incorporate prayer into your daily lives.

I have learned these concepts from my own experiences, and from what I've witnessed from the relationships of those around me. I have been married twice, and widowed twice. The first marriage lasted just under two years, and the second marriage lasted just under fourteen years. Each marriage was unique, and I learned different things from each about communication and about myself. I learned that what works in one marriage, might not work in another marriage. I've learned from my mistakes, and from the mistakes of others, and I want to share these lessons with you.

CHAPTER ONE
The Honeymoon Phase

Well, the wedding is over and now the rest of your life begins. You're in love. But as you lay there on your wedding night, perhaps you're still not sure that you did the right thing. Is it going to last? Did you make the right choice? Did you move too fast and get married too soon? How well do you really know this person? I actually asked myself these questions. I was so nervous. I told myself to think positively.

On the other hand, maybe you're one of those people, like my husband Lamar, who sees nothing but bliss during this phase and you know without a doubt that this was the best decision you ever made. The wedding was perfect. Your bride was beautiful. You can't think of any other place you would rather be in the world than right here by her side. You feel like you were made for each other, and she has made you the happiest person in the world by marrying you.

We are individuals. This means you can have two people looking at the same situation and feeling very differently about it. So we each try to make the best of our new union.

You see, both of us prayed to God asking Him to send the spouse that He wanted us to have. We each listed the qualities that we wanted in a spouse, and waited on God. Then we ran into each other, and soon decided that God had answered our prayers. We discovered we want the same things out of life. We both love the Lord, and want to please Him. We both value the sanctity of marriage.

The honeymoon phase can last for a few months, or even for a few years, although it typically lasts about a year. So what happens when the honeymoon is over? Well, remember how you initially overlooked the little things that annoyed you about your spouse? You love this person, so you figure surely you can excuse a few things that get on your nerves. When the honeymoon is over, you find that those same little things become more annoying. You have a choice: you can discuss these issues with your significant other, or remain silent.

Chapter Two

Marriage After the Honeymoon

Although the actual honeymoon is over, as you get used to living with each other, the honeymoon feel is still there. Sometimes you disagree, but someone always gives in, or compromises, and everything is alright. But what happens when everything is not alright, and the disagreement lingers? This is where your level of communication based on love and respect will be tested.

Men and women are different, and we communicate differently as a result. It's one reason why we tend to have disagreements. You have to learn how to interpret what is actually being said when your spouse expresses their personal desire or point of view. Sometimes the words you hear are not actually what is being said.

Let's look at an example: Gina has an upsetting day at work, and when she gets home, she tells her husband, Steve, all about it. Steve sees that she is upset and he listens as she explains her day. Suddenly he remembers that he is supposed to meet some friends to watch the game, and that the game is about to start. He makes suggestions about what Gina could do the next time she's faced with the same situation, then tells her that he has to go meet some of his friends to watch the game. She says okay. He gives her a hug and leaves. Well, Steve didn't realize that Gina was venting and just wanted to be comforted. He assumed that she was looking for advice. But Gina already knew what to do differently next time, so she wasn't looking for solutions. She simply wanted to talk about what was upsetting her. She expected Steve to listen, and had been looking forward to spending time with him after such a long day at work. He assumed that when she said "okay", she meant it was fine that he was leaving. In reality, when Gina realized that Steve wants to go watch the game, she said "okay" even though she felt upset and disappointed. She would have preferred that he stay home and spend time with her, which she would have viewed as an act of love in this situation. Instead, Steve goes to meet his friends, while Gina is at home feeling unloved.

Here is another example of the importance of open and direct communication: I was in a department store with my husband Lamar. I saw a coat that I liked, but I wished that it came in a darker color. Lamar said that if I liked it, then I should buy it. He offered to buy it for me, but I decided that it was too pale, and would stain easily so I didn't get it. About a month later, a male friend told me he thinks my coat is too thin, and suggested that I get a heavier coat for the winter. I agreed, and told him that I had been looking for a heavier coat. My friend, whom

I had known for years, said that he wanted to contribute to the purchase of my coat as a gift. I went to the store later and continued my search for a coat. I couldn't find one that I liked, so I decided to go ahead and get the one I had seen a month prior. When I got home, Lamar saw the coat and said, "I thought you didn't want that coat because it wasn't dark enough." I explained that I had changed my mind about it because I couldn't find anything else that I liked. I told him about the conversation with my friend about getting a new coat, and mentioned that the friend had given me some money to go toward the purchase as a gift, and that I had paid the difference. Lamar reminded me that he had tried to buy me that coat, but I had said that I didn't want it. Now he was upset, and became completely silent. He probably felt disrespected. I realized that he was upset, so I apologized and tried to explain that it was an innocent situation. I didn't want to offend my friend by not accepting his gift. To me, it was just a coincidence that I purchased that particular coat, but to Lamar, it felt like disrespect.

As these two examples showed, when a woman is disappointed by her spouse, she tends to feel unloved, whereas when a man is disappointed by his wife, he tends to feel disrespected. This is an important concept to understand. If the wife continues to feel unloved, she's unlikely to be motivated to attend to the needs if her husband. Likewise, the husband is unlikely to tend to the wife's needs if he feels disrespected. The key is to figure out how to communicate to minimize these all-too-common responses.

It is so important to ask questions, and not just make assumptions. In both of the examples, assumptions were made. Steve assumed he knew what kind of response Gina wanted, and Gina assumed that Steve would know how she felt without actually saying it. I assumed it would be okay to buy that coat with the money my friend had given me, and I didn't take into consideration how Lamar would feel about it. In hind sight, I should have let Lamar buy me the coat, once I had made up my mind to get it, especially since he had initially offered. Sometimes we manage to do things that are offensive, even when we don't intend to offend. It's kind of two sided. Lamar needed to remember that I wouldn't do something to intentionally offend him, and I needed to look at the situation from his point of view before I purchased that coat. But it wasn't really just about the coat, it's about being considerate in general. Practicing being considerate should help improve any relationship we're in.

Chapter Three

No One Is a Mind Reader

As we saw in the last chapter, communication is a very important issue in a marriage. The lack there of can destroy any relationship. If you have a problem with your spouse, it's best to address the issue as soon as it arises. You should always be completely honest with each other and explain exactly how you feel. Never assume that the other person knows how you feel or what you need. Neither of you is a mind reader. For a while, I had a terrible habit of assuming Lamar knew what I wanted from him. If he had a day off during the week, I assumed that he would do some housework. Wrong! He didn't do any, because he simply wasn't thinking about it. I realized that I made that assumption because that's what *I* would be thinking about if I was at home on my day off. If I wanted him to do the laundry, then I needed to put it in his mind by explicitly asking him to do it.

Sometimes people get defensive when confronted with their flaws. All of a sudden they're walking around with an attitude, and you don't know why. A good way to approach a sensitive issue is to avoid pointing fingers. For example, start by saying, "I don't like it when you…" or "it upsets me when you…" or "I would appreciate it if you…" instead of "why don't you…" or "why do you…" or "why can't you…" The way you approach the topic is just as important as what you want to say to your spouse. Most of the time, when people get defensive, they tend not to hear what you are saying because they are offended by your approach. Once that happens you are unlikely to get your point across, and the conversation is basically over.

Listening is also very important. We have to learn to see things from other people's perspectives. Your opinion matters, but so does the other person's. Even if you disagree with your spouse's point of view, you still need to respect their opinion. Early on in our marriage, if Lamar said something that made no sense to me, I would just dismiss it as being ridiculous. I didn't realize at the time that my response showed a lack of respect for his opinion. I had to learn to be more sensitive to what Lamar was saying. It made sense in his mind, but because he left out certain details, what he was saying made no sense to me. I was guilty of doing the same thing on other occasions. I would think that I had told him something, but I actually hadn't. So our conversation would be based on what I thought I had already told him. For example, if our daughter had a performance at six p.m., at three that afternoon I might say to Lamar, "Can you make sure that Cymone has her red shirt for tonight". Then he would say, "What's happening tonight?" I would then 'remind' him that she had a chorus performance. He would reply that I hadn't told him about it, and when I thought about it, I would realize that he was right.

It's wise to take what the other person is saying seriously. Sometimes the disagreement may be about something you consider to be silly. This happened once with Lamar and me. Something happened and Lamar became offended, but I couldn't understand why since, in my opinion, it wasn't something he should take offense to. Well, he was so upset that he said he needed time away from me, which ended up being a whole month. I eventually learned that just because *I* wouldn't be offended by something, that didn't mean that Lamar shouldn't be offended by it. As this example shows, it's very important to take your spouse's concerns seriously. Not doings so can be detrimental to the relationship.

Sometimes a disagreement could stem from just a simple misunderstanding, which could easily be cleared up through communication. No one can read minds, so it is important to tell the other person exactly what you want them to know. A lack of effective communication leads to unresolved issues. Unresolved issues can eat away at the core of a relationship, sometimes to the point where the relationship cannot be salvaged. This is why it is important to address the issues as soon as possible. Assuming that the other person knows what you want is unwise, and it's unfair to that person when you get upset because they didn't do what you were expecting them to do.

Sometimes the other person's complaint may seem unreasonable to you, but God knows them best. God can read minds. Prayer is one of the best things that you can do for your relationship. Ask God to help you better understand your spouse's point of view, and He will do it. You may be surprised by what He says. While you're praying to gain a better understanding of your spouse, you might want to ask God to help you see the areas where you need improvement. Sometimes it is *you* who needs to change, and not your spouse. In other words, sometimes your wrong, and your spouse is right. Sometimes your both wrong. God will let you know. It is so important to be open to whatever God says to you, especially since we don't always realize when we're wrong.

Sometimes it takes God to show us, so we can change for the better. We are all a work in progress; none of us are perfect. It's okay to be wrong. The problem arises when you know that you're wrong and you're not willing to change.

I have found that it helps to write down the things that bother you. It's best to do this when you are not upset. On a few occasions, Lamar and I each listed the things we wanted the other to person to improve upon, and the things the other person did that upset us. Then we exchanged our lists. The idea was that we would both work on the things that the other person had a problem with.

Some people benefit from writing down the things they want to say while they are upset, as opposed to arguing in the heat of the moment. This practice minimizes arguing, and allows you to get your point across without being interrupted. The information that gets written down can also be used to help you remember what was said during the 'argument', since some people get so upset during the disagreement that they forget what exactly was said.

CHAPTER FOUR

Mind Your Mouth: Once You Say It, You Can't Take It Back

Arguing solves nothing. It just creates tension and opens the door for walls to be put up between a couple. It can take years to tear down emotional walls, which is a whole other issue. Arguing can lead to acting out of anger, and the end result can be damaging. Once you say something, you can't take it back. If you are angry and you feel hurtful words coming to the surface, just leave the room. Do something else to distract yourself from the anger. Anger is a natural reaction in certain situations, but it's acting out of anger that's the problem.

People tend to bring up past hurts or disappointments during arguments. We must learn to leave the past in the past. Of course you won't forget about what happened in the past, but you can't allow yourself to dwell on it. This can be very harmful to your relationship. The best thing to do with the past is to learn from it and move on with your life. Whatever your spouse did to hurt your feelings, let them know, and then try not to bring it up again. That was hard for me to do, because I felt so disappointed by whatever had happened, and I just couldn't get over it. Especially if it was something Lamar continued to do, knowing that it irritated me. Being able to let things go is necessary for growth in your relationship. It doesn't matter how often the offense is repeated. This is the essence of forgiveness and unconditional love. I had to keep in mind he wasn't being malicious, or intentionally trying to irritate me or hurt my feelings. That makes a difference.

When a spouse does something hurtful, most people's initial reaction is to become defensive. This is when forgiveness can bring peace in your relationship. There are two things to take into consideration. Number one: your spouse wouldn't do things to intentionally hurt you. If it seems like they did something on purpose, it's possible that a misunderstanding has taken place. For example, I had been planning to go to a baby shower that started at five, and I told Lamar that I needed him to be home by then so that I could get there by five thirty at the latest. Our children were small at the time, and I didn't want to take them with me. I reminded him several times (a week before, then the day before, then that morning). Well, five o'clock came and went and Lamar wasn't home yet. I tried calling him a couple of times but I got his voice mail. At six he called and said that he was on the way home. I expressed my frustration, and reminded him that I was supposed to be at the shower by now. He just stated that he would be home soon. Then at six thirty, Lamar pulled into the driveway. I was fuming. I assumed he forgot, or lost track of time (which were a few of his bad habits). It turns out that he didn't forget. He was helping one of his customers with their car repair and the person had an emergency, causing Lamar to be delayed. He felt tired, and frustrated that the job had caused him to be delayed. He knew that I was mad, and he didn't want to argue about it on the phone. The situation was beyond his control, but I didn't know that.

The second thing to consider is that no one is perfect. We all make mistakes. There's nothing wrong with feeling hurt by something that your spouse did or said. Being able to keep the peace has a lot to do with how you respond to a mistake. Sometimes we pass judgement, become angry, and then act out of anger saying hurtful things that we can't take back. Forgiveness has a way of freeing you, which strengthens you and helps you to move on with your life.

    Sometimes the things that you say or do can cause tension in your relationship. An example of a situation that can cause tension is comparing your spouse to someone else you know. You must remember that we are all individuals with different backgrounds and different life experiences that have shaped who we are. Trying to get your spouse to act like someone else is never the answer. You have to accept them for who they are, and not who you want them to be.

"Even a fool, when he holdeth his peace, is counted wise: and he that shutteth his lips is esteemed a man of understanding." (Proverbs 17:28)

Chapter Five

Pick Your Battles

One thing that we all must consider, in any type of relationship, is when to stand up for your point of view, and when to just take a step back and be quiet. Yes, you must pick your battles. Sometimes you need to decide if the disagreement is important enough to upset your spouse. You may be right, and they may be wrong, but is getting your way worth the hurt you might cause? It depends on the issue. If the issue is a deal breaker, such as something that compromises your morals, then stand your ground. If it's something that won't matter tomorrow, then let it go. You might be surprised to find that your spouse might come around to seeing the situation from your point of view once they've had time to think about it. If not, that's okay too. Keep in mind that there's more than one right way to do most things. You may have the same goal, but just different ideas about how to achieve that goal.

One way to minimize some of these battles is to get to know your spouse better. This involves patience. It takes time to understand your spouse's personality, and what they can tolerate. Some people are more sensitive than others and can handle a situation better if they are told the main point minus the details. Other people will understand the situation better if they are given all the details. Some arguments can easily be avoided if you learn what to say and when to say it. It would benefit you to ask God to help you know when to speak versus when to keep quiet and just pray.

Remember that women and men communicate differently, and have different needs. For women, love has several parts. For example, women desire closeness, responsiveness, and understanding, all of which makes them feel loved. Sometimes women can seem negative and/or offensive to men. A lot of times this is a reaction to not receiving the love that is desired. For example, if Chris, the husband, spends most of his time doing things that don't include Pam, his wife, then she may feel neglected. This feeling of neglect leads to a desire for closeness. Pam might complain about them not spending enough time together, which could translate to Chris as an annoyance. Here's the other side of this example: Chris is busy trying to finish several projects by a deadline, so he has less time to spend with Pam. He may be annoyed by her complaints because he wants to get his work done and he's already explained this to her. Now, if Chris better understood why Pam reacted the way she did, then he might take this opportunity to pick his battles. Pam would have to express her feelings of neglect so Chris is aware of how she feels. Once he is made aware, he could try to find a way to spend time with her, even if it's just thirty minutes a day. A situation like this could turn into an argument, or an opportunity to nurture the relationship.

For men, their sense of self-worth revolves around respect, which has several parts. For example, men have the desire to protect, provide, and lead, all of which makes them feel respected. Making negative comments or not showing appreciation for their efforts in any of these areas will likely offend your husband. "Nevertheless let everyone of you in particular so love his wife even as himself; and the wife see that she reverence her husband." (Ephesians 5:33)

So what do you do when your spouse won't budge or compromise on an issue that is important to you? It really depends on the situation, and their reason for not compromising. For example, if you are ready to have a child, but your spouse is not. Why does your spouse not want to have a child right now? You have to look at the situation from each other's perspective. If their reason doesn't make any sense to you, then I would advise you to pray about it. Maybe there is an underlying issue that even your spouse isn't aware of, or an issue that they haven't revealed to you. Or maybe you just need clarification. It's not always easy to see things from the perspective of others, which is one reason why prayer is a good option. God can help you to understand the situation, and it usually requires patience. After you pray, you have to wait for the answer. While you are waiting to hear from God, you can agree to disagree. There's nothing wrong with that, and it's never a good idea to force someone to make a major life-changing decision before they're ready.

"Be still, and know that I am God."
(Psalm 46:10)

Chapter Six

Putting In Work: Compromise, Quality Time, and Intimacy

People hardly ever discuss the fact that marriage is like a job. In order to get something out of it, you have to put something into it. You and your spouse are two unique individuals sharing the same space. You have to work to make sure that both of your needs are met. Compromise is necessary in order to successfully share a space and help a marriage last. At times, you have to consider doing some of the things that your spouse enjoys even if it's not something that you may enjoy. For example, maybe your spouse likes going to ball games and you don't. Or you enjoy going to the movies, but your spouse doesn't. Maybe you could agree to go to one game once a month during the game season and your spouse could agree to go to one movie a month in return. Now, don't agree to do something that's a deal breaker for you. For example, anything that you feel may compromise your religious beliefs is a deal breaker.

Spending quality time with each other helps your relationship to grow. You have to set aside time to be in each other's presence when there are no distractions, like the TV. Spending time face to face is necessary. This means actually looking at each other and giving your undivided attention to the other person. I used to think that just being in the same room with your spouse was considered spending quality time even if we were silently watching a movie together. Lamar didn't see that as quality time, though. His definition involved giving the other person your undivided attention.

If you have a busy schedule which makes it difficult to spend quality time with your spouse, then you might consider scheduling date nights. It's a good idea to go on dates anyway. They give you something to look forward to doing together outside the house. Your marriage should always be a priority; it requires your attention so that it can grow and last.

Quality time also includes intimacy. If you and your spouse are too busy to make time for intimacy, then you've got to be creative. During the week, Lamar and I would plan to make time for each other after the kids went to bed, which is one example. If the kids fell asleep in our bed, then Lamar would pick them up and take them to their own beds. The kids were not allowed to sleep in the bed with us, because that would make any attempt at intimacy more difficult.

Compromise also plays a part when it comes to intimacy. For example, you may not always be in the mood when your spouse is in the mood. Not every couple has this issue, but if you do, you are not alone. If your marriage is experiencing intimacy issues, then you might have to be creative. You and your spouse have to figure out a way to meet each other's needs, and this also requires communication. Let your spouse know exactly what your needs are so that they are not left guessing. Having an open discussion about your likes and dislikes will help improve this area of your lives.

A couple can experience different forms of intimacy that don't involve sex. Hugging, kissing, holding hands, and cuddling are some examples of various forms of intimacy. Showing affection in these ways is great for deepening the connection in a relationship. You should have some type of physical contact with your spouse every day. Whenever Lamar or I, would leave for work in the morning, we would give each other a kiss, even if one of us was still asleep (the kiss would wake me or him, but that was fine). We also always gave each other a hug when one of us came home from work, which was a sign of affection. We both enjoyed this display of affection and looked forward to it.

There is a such thing as being overly affectionate, so you have to communicate your level of comfort to your spouse. On the other hand, some people tend not to show affection at all, while others prefer not to show a lot of affection in public. The definition of too much or too little affection is subjective. What you might consider to be too much affection might be not enough for someone else. It just depends on the person. Try to respect your spouse's boundaries, and work out a compromise, if necessary.

It's also important that you take time out for yourself. Go hang out with your friends, or do things that you enjoy doing without your spouse. For example, if your spouse doesn't like shopping, then go shopping by yourself. Just remember that you also have to allow your spouse to have their "me" time. It is important to continue to do some of the things that you enjoyed before you became a couple, even if your spouse has no interest in those things. Being married doesn't mean that you have to lose yourself.

Chapter Seven

Gender Roles

Gender roles can play an important part in the success of a relationship. Now, this doesn't mean that the old-fashioned idea that women should do all the cooking, cleaning, and child rearing is ideal for a relationship, although some people have no problem with that type of arrangement if it works for them. When it comes to gender roles, there should be a balance that both you and your spouse are comfortable with. Discuss your expectations with your spouse and try to find common ground.

In accordance with the Bible, one thing is for sure: there can only be one leader. "Wives, submit yourselves unto your own husbands, as unto the Lord." (Ephesians 5:22) This doesn't mean that a woman can't be independent, and strong; it just means that there is a natural order in a relationship, which God himself has put into place. "For the husband is the head of the wife, even as Christ is the head of the church…" (Ephesians 5:23) Yes ladies, that means that the man is the head of the household, whether you like it or not. It doesn't mean that the husband is always right, but it does mean that he is the leader. Many relationships fail because the wife doesn't allow the husband to take the lead and be the leader. If there is a decision to be made, and I don't agree with Lamar's decision, I still go along with it for this reason. I need to make a clarification. This is specifically related to situations when a couple can't seem to compromise, and the issue is not a deal breaker.

For example, I once wanted to buy some furniture for the living room. Lamar suggested that I wait and save up the money for it instead of financing the purchase. It was one of those deals where you didn't have to pay anything for eighteen months, which I thought was a great idea, and I had been wanting to buy this furniture for a few years now. I just knew that I would end up paying that furniture off before the 18 months was over, and I talked Lamar into coming with me to buy it. Long story short, I ended up paying almost twice as much as the furniture was actually worth. Every time I tried to make a payment, something important would come up and I would have to use the money for that instead. So not only did I not make any early payments, but I also had to pay the high interest rate when I was finally able to start making the payments. That was a hard, expensive lesson related to being obedient to God's word.

If the husband wants to open the door for his wife, she should let him. If he wants to fix things around the house, his wife shouldn't call in a professional; she should let him fix the things when he can. Whenever something major like the fridge wasn't working, I was quick to suggest calling in a professional. Lamar would give me a look like I had lost my mind, and then he would go fix it.

Sometimes it's hard to relinquish control over certain things, especially when you're used to being independent. When I was single, I handled everything myself. When I got married, I had to consider my spouse's opinion before making certain decisions. It took time, patience, and practice to get used to these changes. When my ideas clashed with Lamar's, where we couldn't seem compromise, I had to make a choice. We could go with his idea, or I could do my own thing. I've heard people use the word "submission" when it comes to husbands and wives in this situation. I never really liked that word; it sounded so dated to me. Eventually I realized that what the word means comes down to perspective. Submission is not about obedience; it's about having love and respect in a relationship. I view it as giving my consent, which is me saying, "Sure we can go with your idea". That sounds so much better to me. My mindset had to change from "me" and "I" and "mine" to "we" and "us" and "ours". This is a major adjustment to make.

    The husband has a responsibility to take care of his family. A wise husband will communicate with his wife and consider her opinion before making important decisions. Being the head of the household doesn't mean that you know everything. You and your spouse are partners in life. Being the head of the household means protecting, encouraging, and guiding. Sometimes the wrong choice is made, but that's a part of life. Learning from your mistakes and exercising compromise is the key.

Sometimes God communicates things to the husband, that He does not communicate to the wife. This means that decisions are sometimes made and the wife might not understand why her husband made that choice. If this results in a disagreement, then I would encourage the husband to trust God and do what God has instructed him to do. There were times when I didn't agree with Lamar's decision and he ended up being right. He listened to God and made the right choice, despite my objection. When I came to realize that his choice was a result of his interaction with God, I was grateful that he hadn't let me persuade him to make the opposite choice. For this reason, I encourage husbands to let God deal with the wife's objection, and pray that God will give her an understanding about the necessity of the choice.

The key word when it comes to this type of decision-making is "sometimes". The idea for every choice that you make doesn't necessarily come from God. Husbands, you live and you learn. Listening for Gods instruction comes easily for some, but for others, it takes practice. Our own thoughts and ideas can get in the way, making it more difficult to hear what God is saying. Another word for this is "distraction", or even "pride".

One thing to keep in mind is that women and men are just different. We think differently, and respond differently to the same situations. This is why we have gender roles. We must learn to accept our differences. I'm not talking about the deal breakers, like abusive behavior. I'm talking about accepting someone for who they are, and learning to adjust to having another individual living in your space.

"Trust in the Lord with all thine heart; and lean not to thine own understanding. In all thy ways acknowledge him, and he shall direct thy paths." (Proverbs 3:5,6)

Chapter Eight

For Better or For Worse

Marriage is about taking the good with the bad. After you get married, your perspective of your spouse might change. Just being married changes the dynamic of your relationship, even if you lived together before marriage. Adjusting to shared decision-making and having to be accountable to someone else takes time. It may be uncomfortable at times, especially when you don't agree with each other, but this is where patience and compromise will benefit you.

The balance of give and take is important to consider. Marriage is a two-way street. If one person is always taking and hardly ever giving, this can lead to resentment from the spouse doing the giving. An example of this is when one spouse gets to frequently do the things they like doing, while their spouse hardly ever gets to do things they enjoy. One way to avoid this conflict is to communicate. Also, if it seems that the two of you are usually doing the things that you like, plan activities that you know your spouse would enjoy. If you're not sure what those are, just ask them. Even if your spouse has no complaints, and doesn't seem to mind doing the things that you like. They would probably still appreciate you making the effort to include some of the things they enjoy when you are together. Being considerate goes a long way in any relationship. One characteristic of love is simply doing things for the well-being of the person you love, and not expecting anything in return.

    Another aspect in which you must take the good with the bad involves strengths and weaknesses. We all have them, and over time you will learn what those are for your spouse. This is an opportunity for you to grow together. In areas where you're weak, your spouse should support you. Weakness can come in different forms. Maybe you are high-strung and your spouse is more laid-back. Or maybe your spouse is awful at budgeting and you are great at it. Use these differences to help support each other and grow as a couple.

Communication, trust, consideration, and patience are all important when it comes to dealing with the issue of strengths and weaknesses. If the weakness is something that requires counseling or support groups, do what you can to encourage your spouse to seek the help they need. One important thing to remember is that God can make us strong where we are weak. Pray for your spouse, and encourage them to pray for themselves as well. While prayer may not stop a person from doing what they intend to do, it can decrease temptation and strengthen their resolve. God can help you, and He *will* help you if you ask for it. "Ask, and it shall be given unto you... For everyone that asketh receiveth..." (Matthew 7:7,8). "The Lord will give strength unto his people; the Lord will bless his people with peace." (Psalm 29:11)

It's also important that you not judge your spouse, especially when they're not at their best. Some people don't realize that they take more than they give. Maybe they're used to being given things all the time, so they don't think about it. Some people have a hard time improving upon their weaknesses. Maybe they haven't had much support in the past, or maybe they just haven't explored all their options for overcoming the weakness. Try not to rush them, or force the progression of change. Allow your spouse to grow at their own pace so they don't resent you for what can be considered passing judgement. Just encourage them and praise their accomplishments. Encouragement requires empathy and looking at the world from your spouse's perspective.

One topic to consider when we talk about the good with the bad is the past. In a relationship, you trust that your spouse has shared whatever you feel you need to know about their past. Sometimes things that happened in the past, both known to you and unknown to you, may become a topic of discussion. If the information is not a deal breaker, or has no effect on your current relationship, then you should let it go. It was in the past. Dwelling on the past can damage your relationship. We all have a past, and once again, no one is perfect. Love diminishes when you focus on the negative.

Conversely, love grows when we focus on the positive.

"Brethren, I count not myself to have apprehended: but this one thing I do, forgetting those things which are behind, and reaching forth unto those things which are before…" (Philippians 3:13)

CHAPTER NINE

Outside Influences

Sometimes situations or people outside the home can cause problems within your relationship. Family members, friends, even your job can all interfere to a point that damages your relationship. Whenever you involve family and friends in your home life, it's wise to stick to the positive things about your relationship. There are two reasons for this. First, if you vent to a family member or a friend about your spouse, they're unlikely to be as forgiving as you are. For example, you have an argument with your spouse, so you vent to your sister about it. Later, you and your spouse make up. Well, now your sister is upset about the way your spouse treated you and has a negative view of your spouse, even if you tell her that you've made up with your spouse. You have moved on, but she has not. This will likely effect how your sister treats your spouse from now on. The best way to avoid this situation is to keep your family and friends out of your relationship business.

The second reason to not talk negatively about your spouse to others is that they may continue to bring up the negative information in the future. They may even be so bold as to mention their point of view about the issue to your spouse the next time they see them. One main exception to this is if you feel that your life or wellbeing is being threatened, and you need to talk to someone about it. Then please do.

It's a good idea to discuss the role that in-laws will play in your lives. You should discuss how you feel about them visiting and about how involved they will be in your daily lives. It helps if you settle this issue before it becomes a problem. This is not the time to make assumptions, especially if they are not just coming for a visit, but they are coming to live with you for whatever reason. It's important to explore how you both would feel about that situation before it happens. Just give it some thought, so that if it does happen, at least you have an idea about what you expect the situation to be like. Keep in mind that this can be a very sensitive topic for some people. Having a major difference of opinion in this area can have a detrimental effect on your marriage.

    I experienced a challenge like this when Lamar asked if his mom, who lived in a different state, could come and live with us. At the time, she was living with her sister and they weren't getting along. So I said it was fine. I assumed she was coming to stay with us until she got a job and got on her feet. This was not the case. She was coming to stay with us indefinitely, and she was not planning on getting a job. Lamar knew this, but didn't share that info with me. I didn't ask about the specifics; I just made assumptions. I have no idea why he chose not to share that important information with me. This break in communication resulted in an uncomfortable situation for all of us.

One thing to keep in mind is that your spouse comes before your family members. When you get married, you become as one. "For this cause shall a man leave his father and mother, and shall be joined unto his wife, and they two shall be one flesh." (Ephesians 5:31) It doesn't mean that your family isn't important; it just means that out of all your relationships, your spouse comes first.

If there's a dispute involving your spouse and your family members, it's a good idea for you to be the one to deal with your family members. You know them better than your spouse does, and you know what you should say to them and how you should say it. You are the mediator, and your family is more likely to accept constructive criticism from you than from your spouse (especially if your family member is out of line). This will also help your spouse feel more comfortable, and help minimize misunderstandings.

Jobs are another situation that can interfere with your relationship. If a job prevents you from being able to spend quality time with your spouse, this can present a problem. Your spouse is the priority. If your job is demanding, try to work your spouse into your weekly schedule.

Finances, money, and/or bills can all be the cause of arguments and have a negative influence on your relationship when you disagree about how to manage them. I suggest using a financial counselor to help you sort through your finances. They can also help you plan your financial future. A financial planner is an objective third party who is unlikely to take sides and instead, state the facts as they are presented.

As for what to do about the day-to-day issues, like paying bills and making purchases, you have to discuss them with each other. What works for one couple might not work for another. One approach is to agree upon an amount that you can't exceed unless you speak with your spouse about the purchase first. You might benefit from having a joint account that is specifically for paying bills and maintaining separate accounts for personal use.

It's also important to know about each other's debts. One way to ensure that both spouses have full disclosure is by exchanging credit reports. By doing this, you can both see what needs to be addressed financially and prioritize accordingly. It's also a good idea for you and your spouse to know what's going on with the finances in case something happens to one of you, like a long term medical issue or a death.

One thing to consider when it comes to money is unequal incomes. If one spouse makes significantly more than the other, then the spouse who makes less should contribute less financially. For example, since I made more than Lamar, I didn't expect him to pay the same amount as I paid towards the bills. It just didn't seem fair to me. Also, I don't agree with the idea that the man is responsible for paying all the bills no matter the situation; because we are a team. That might not work for you, or maybe it would. It's not always fair to split things 50/50, especially in the example that I gave. I didn't think any less of Lamar in that example either. Some guys feel that they have to do it all, even if their wife makes more, simply because they believe it's the man's responsibility. Some women believe that too. It just seems like unnecessary pressure on the person who makes less.

Infidelity involves an outside influence that definitely would interfere with your relationship. There are two types of cheating: emotional and physical. I would describe emotional cheating as when a married person spends time, usually one on one, with someone that they are attracted to in a social, intimate way. I'm not talking about spending long hours at work with someone you happen to find attractive, if you're actually working. I'm talking about hanging out with the person that you're attracted to, or phone conversations that you know your spouse would not appreciate, if they knew about it.

Remember back in the day when men and women weren't allowed to be alone together if they weren't married? They had to have a chaperone. Well, there was reason for that. People didn't want to give the impression that something inappropriate was going on between them, and it was considered unwise to be in the company of the opposite sex alone. Temptation is real. The best thing to do is to avoid putting yourself in a position in which you are alone with someone you are attracted to. There's nothing wrong with finding someone attractive. Allowing your thoughts to go in inappropriate directions involving that person is the problem. Cheating starts in the mind. From there it can progress to the physical act of cheating.

Physical cheating is when you have sexual relations, of any kind, with someone other than your spouse. Just because one spouse cheats doesn't make it okay for the other one to do the same. Two wrongs don't make a right. Depending on the person and the situation, a marriage can still be salvaged after infidelity has occurred. For some people, cheating is a deal breaker that ends the marriage.

For others, the length of time that they've been married makes a difference in determining what will happen next. For example, if you've been married for several years and you both want the marriage to work, then you might be able to save it. On the other hand, if one spouse wants the marriage to end, then that marriage might not be saved. There are a lot of variables, and once again, what works for some might not work for others.

Chapter Ten

Always Give Praise and Show Appreciation

One important issue that people tend to neglect, is giving praise. A relationship benefits greatly when you both give credit where it is due and show appreciation for each other. When someone goes out of their way to do something that benefits the marriage, the other spouse should let them know that they are appreciated. Even if it's something that you would expect them to do anyway, you should still get in the habit of showing your gratitude. Saying "thank you" is a start. Explaining to your spouse exactly why you appreciate their efforts goes a long way. Showing them that you are grateful for their consideration is also a plus. This can be done in many different ways, just use your imagination.

No one likes to feel that they are not appreciated. Whether their act was a life changer or just something that lifted your spirits, always take the time to express your appreciation. Don't take your spouse for granted. Treat each other like it's a privilege to be married to one another.

Chapter Eleven

Incorporate the Fruits of the Spirit Into Your Relationship

One way to greatly improve the quality of your relationship is to incorporate the fruits of the spirit into your daily lives. According to Galatians 5:22-23, the fruits of the spirit are love, joy, peace, longsuffering, gentleness, goodness, faith, meekness, and temperance. Let's take a look at how these fruits relate to your relationship. Love your spouse as you do yourself. Being happy and not dwelling on negativity or sadness is the essence of joy. Live peacefully with each other to the best of your ability. A part of longsuffering involves bearing each other's burdens for as long as it takes to overcome the issue. This means that you have each other's backs. Gentleness is to handle each other with care, and be sensitive to each other's feelings. Goodness is simply just being nice and trying to do what's right. Believing that no matter what the situation looks like, God is in control, and that everything happens for a reason is the essence of faith. Meekness is to humble yourself and be servants to each other. Temperance is being patient with each other and exercising self-control in all things. If you strive to incorporate these qualities into your lives, your chances of staying happily married will be greatly improved.

Conclusion

We've seen how effective communication is a major contributor to the success of your marriage. No one is a mind reader. You have to be willing to share your desires, and openly discuss what makes you uncomfortable. You must be considerate of your spouse's comfort level and their boundaries. Having patience with each other is important when dealing with your differences, and compromise is a necessity in all areas of your marriage. You have to be willing to make sacrifices for each other.

You have to want to communicate in a way that is respectful and loving. You're responsible for your responses. Remember that it's not always what you say, but how you say it, and that once you say something you can never take it back. When you're faced with an issue that causes a dispute, the idea should be to attack the issue and not each other. You're a team and no matter what, you should always have each other's backs. Don't give up on each other.

To have a healthy marriage, you need to put in some work. This requires spending quality time with each other, showing affection, and making time for intimacy. Your spouse and your marriage have to be the priority in your life. We're all individuals, and no one is perfect. Taking the good with the bad is expected in a marriage. If you need help getting through the bad, God is always there. (It's also a good idea to acknowledge God when things are going well in your relationship.) God knows you better than you know yourself, so it would be wise to consult him whenever you need guidance or strength. Prayer and a positive attitude are the key. When we go through tough times, it's your attitude during that time that matters most. Prayer won't change the fact that you will experience trials in your relationship, but prayer can help you to maintain a positive frame of mind during those trials.

Remember to keep people out of your business. Try not to say negative things about your spouse to other people, and never fight in public. When you are frustrated with your spouse, try to think about the things that you like most about them. Think about the things that you appreciate about them. I made a list of the things that I appreciated about Lamar so that when I was upset, I could go back and read them to remind myself of the positive things about him. It's not easy to think about these things off of the top of your head when you're mad at someone, so having the list helped me. Doing this changes your mindset from a negative one to a positive one.

Make sure you take the time to let your spouse know that you appreciate them. Everyone likes to feel appreciated, and it helps your spouse to know that they are doing things that make you happy. Don't just assume that they know that you appreciate them. If all they ever hear are the things they are doing wrong, or the things you don't like, then how will they know you appreciate them? You have to tell them.

Finally, taking the time to incorporate the fruits of the spirit into your life will help you nourish and grow your relationship. This way of life should allow you to be more open to the needs of your spouse, and to the plan that God has for your life. The goal is not to get your spouse to do what you want them to do, but rather to release them to God so he can get them to do what he wants them to do. Think about that for a minute. If you and your spouse allow yourselves to be lead by God, your relationship will flourish.

Acknowledgements

Giving all honor to God; I would like to thank him for allowing me to share this message with you. God has given me the strength and the courage to complete this book so that someone's life and relationship may be changed for the better. No matter what we face in life, God is there. I thank him for being my rock, my provider, my friend, my counselor, my mind regulator, and my comforter.

I want to thank my mom for being an example of courage and strength. I thank God for her and I pray that she will continue to let God's light shine through her wherever she goes.

To my beta reader: Eugene Allington, thank you for your encouragement, input, and critique. I greatly appreciate you.

I thank Kenn Bivins for taking the time to give his advice and for sharing his marketing experience.

I want to thank Sondra, Tina, Fristine and Clarrissa for their insight and the knowledge they shared.

To you, my readers: I am grateful that you chose to allow me to share this message with you. Thank you for your support and I pray that God will continue to bless you in your relationships.

Please let me know how this book has helped you by emailing me at <u>deven_jones@yahoo.com</u>

You can also visit my blog at devenspov.com for upcoming events and for additional words of encouragement.

Follow me on Instagram @ devenbjones

Things that I appreciate about my spouse…

Things that I can work on to improve our relationship…

_____

_____

_____

_____

_____

_____

_____

_____

_____

_____

_____

_____

_____

_____

Things that *you* feel I should work on to improve our relationship…

Additional notes

www.ingramcontent.com/pod-product-compliance
Lightning Source LLC
Chambersburg PA
CBHW051658040426
42446CB00009B/1190